I0502642

MAKING MONEY
WHILE SLEEPING

10 Passive Income Ideas + a Bonus

Miguel Dos Anjos

Contents

INTRODUCTION

L ife is short and we need to make the best out of it. People have told me in the past I was greedy, or too much money focused. Well, aren't we all money focused?! Most people don't realize, but we study our entire early lives so we can get a 9 to 5 job to pay for our car, our house, and the nice things we want. While school has being teaching us so many things, so one day we can get a degree, school entirely skips the concept of financial intelligence.

While we can have the best job out there, with the highest paying, without financial intelligence we still can't get far ahead. In order to be truly successful on the long run we need to live below our means. Most people after getting a nice paying job will go out, and buy a car, when they get a pay raise, they will buy a bigger house, and in every corner in life whenever the money income increases they will find a way to allocate that money into a liability. Yes, your car and your house are liabilities, because they cost insurance, taxes, maintenance, and constantly take money out of your pocket. The secret to this formula is to invest in assets. Assets are everything that put money in your pocket, a high yield savings account, a rented real estate unit, or a good dividend stock are some examples of assets.

Many very successful young athletes that make millions in their early career lives end up broke exactly where they started once the money stops coming in. Coming from a poor background, nobody told them to invest the money, instead they spend it all in liabilities. No pile of money is big enough to last forever without assets, and an educated resource allocation. Same thing for people who win the jackpot, the money comes fast, and easy, and just as fast goes easy. Being poor once again they will blame the system, or blame the rich, never realizing their own lack of financial knowledge.

In this book we will cover some of my favorite assets, and investments. And my favorite ones are the ones also called "Passive Income" assets. Which means that there is work required up front, but once it is set up, and stablished, minimal to none work is needed to keep it running.

CHAPTER 1: HIGH APY SAVINGS ACCOUNTS

Money that is just standing is money being wasted. Money needs to be always working for us. In the USA we have an average of 3% inflation a year. Every year if we just save the money under our mattress the money will lose 3% of its buying power by the end of the year. For the money to have the same buying power year after year it has to grow at least 3%. This is an inflation percentage average; this year inflation may be 2%, and next year it might turn to be 4%.

Banks are always offering new promotions savings accounts with high yield per year interest to attract new customers. A great benefit of most savings account is that you can take your money out any time you want in case you need it. Always search for the best deals out there, many times banks will offer you a great deal hoping you end up using them for other services as well, or just letting the bank use your money as they wish while you don't need it.

At the moment I'm writing this book, May 2019, I hold 2 high APY savings accounts, each for a specific reason. DCU, Digital Federal Credit Union has an online savings account with 6.17% APY (Annual Percentage Yield), one reason they can afford to create good deals other banks cannot is because they are mostly an online bank that do not need to pay for all the costs of having buildings in every location they want to provide theirs business. For the account I have with DCU there is one catch: it is only for your first $1,000 after that the interest drops to .25%. Don't tell anybody but I transferred $900 to that account, and I intend on not letting it go above $1k. Before reaching $1k I'll simply make a $50 payment from that account, and let it grow for another year. Fifty dollars a year is not a whole lot, but since this money is just saved for the case of an emergency it works great for me. Not to mention that after setting it up I need to do nothing else, but simply collect a $5 monthly credit. I do usually login once a month to all my accounts to see if all is well, which takes me less than a minute a month.

I will cover how to profit from using credit cards on chapter 3, but after opening your new high APY savings account if the bank you choose to open your account with allows; make the deposit with your cash back credit card, and instantly at the moment you open the account, and make the deposit with your cash back credit card you will be entitled to $9 - $45 depending on how much cash back percentage your credit card gives you. Only do this if you have the cash to open the account at that moment, and make sure you pay the credit card in full at the end of the monthly billing cycle to prevent the credit card company from collecting interest off of you. As we will cover in chapter 3, collecting 5% cash back is only good if you always pay your credit card in full at the end of each monthly billing cycle to prevent the credit card company from charging you 25% interest.

For the moment another of my favorite savings account is a 360 Money Market savings account with Capital 1, this account allows you to touch the money at any time you need to, and the interest they provide at the moment is 2% APY. It's better than most banks that will give you .02% APY, still 2% is not perfect but, when I opened the account in January 2019, if you had a minimum X amount of money that you did not need for a certain period of time, and could afford to leave it sitting in the account for a month or so, Capital 1 gave a $200 gift. At first I was wondering if they would follow throw with that promise but they did and I'm very happy with them. The $200 promotion I believe ended, but different banks constantly come up with new promotions, and offers to attract new clients. Do your research at the time you are ready to open your account, and choose the one that best fits your specific needs.

In the past I've had a savings account called "Pot of Gold" with Crown Bank. That account provided a 3% APY, sadly this account is no longer offered. Be sure to look for the best savings accounts out there instead of letting your money sit in an account like Bank of America that often offers .02% APY. Two to six percent is ok for an investment considering there is no risk involved. Usually, higher the risk involved higher is the return.

Another option you can take a look out there are CD's (Certificate of Deposit) account. They will take your money, and usually not let you touch it for an amount of time you decide to let them have it, with a higher interest return. Many times they will let you take your money back in case of an emergency, but you might need to pay a penalty, so make sure if you do put money in a CD, you will not need that money any time soon. Also, the longer you agree to leave your money in the CD account, the higher the APY they will give you. I have not personally, chosen this option for now, because I am ok with higher risks investments that provide higher returns.

For the most part a high APY savings account is great for you to keep your emergency fund, since it is easy to access it. When searching for a good savings account it took me many hours of searching, studying, and reading small letters, but once I found the ideal accounts for me, opening each account took 30 minutes. Also, it is worth mentioning that each month the interest compounds; meaning that each following month the interest will be a little higher than the previous month since you get to collect the interest on top of last month's interest.

STOCK MARKET

Chapter 2.1: The Stock Market/Overview

With no doubt this is my favorite investment, because there is so much potential. By buying stocks we become owners of a corporation, with one stock or even many stocks we are still very very small owners, but nonetheless owners of that company.

To buy the stock we will need an investing account/platform. For somebody just starting it is ideal to find a platform that will not charge high broker fees when buying, or selling a stock, such as Robinhood, currently free of broker fees, MerrylEdge will provide a certain amount of free trades as long as you have above a specific amount average money to invest with them. The reason to make sure, and study the best platform for you to start investing is to avoid having all your gains obtained in stocks being taken away from you in the form of broker trading fees.

There are different ways to make money on the stock market. The most famous way is to buy the stock, for example for $100, and with time the company, and the stock will grow in value, and by the time you sell that stock in this example let's say the stock is now worth $115, resulting in a $15 profit on the share.

Another way to make money on the stock market is to buy stocks that pay dividends. The company will pay you a percentage of their profits. Usually as the company grow the dividend payment will grow as well, and similarly if the company starts facing harder times, or for any other reason decides to, may decrease, or stop paying dividends.

All stock strategies will usually vary from 3 primary, different approaches:

1- Day Trading:

Investors will buy stocks, and hold it for very short amounts of time, a day, an hour, or even minutes, sell it, and try to make a small quick profit.

2- Swing Trading:

A swing trader will usually buy a stock, and hold it for 2 to 6 days, and make the profit based on knowledge of an event that will happen, such as; a release of a new great product, and result in a positive outcome that will grow that stock.

3- Long Term Buying:

This is the best fit for most investors, because we can buy the stock, and hold it for longer periods of time; months, a year, or 10 years allowing time for the stock to grow.

CHAPTER 2.2: STOCK MARKET CURRENT SITUATION

As I'm writing this book we are on May 2019. This is a very specific time to be in, because every 5 to 7 years average a certain degree of recession hits the market. When this hard times hit is when many companies die out, many people lose lots of money, but, also after the recession hits is the time that we see which were/are the strongest companies. At this point an opportunity opens for those who are able to see it coming, prepare for it, and make lots, and lots of money.

The last recession happened in 2008, and from 2009 to 2019 we have been enjoying this bull (growth) market 10 years now. It is not a question of "if", but "when" the next recession will hit, but eventually it will hit. For the last 5 months, for example, the market seems to be inflated similarly to when the real state bubble busted in 2008. There are talks of growth being partially fake related to stock manipulation. Some people say the market is also enjoying a sugar rush from recent government short term tax cuts.

And another huge sign that things may soon change is the inverted yield curve (negative yield curve). This means that when buying bonds you get a smaller return on longer term investing, which normally does not make sense. If your money is trapped longer the return should be higher. All this show a clear sign of complication to come. For the last over 100 years every time the yield bond curve inverted a recession followed within 2 months to 2 years. Every one of this times people said that that time was different and the outcome would be different, and every time the outcome was the same.

The US market has every time come back, going up wards about 71% of the time in the last 130 years. This means that the stock market is a good investment on the longer run. Usually it is not a good idea to invest money that you will need, tomorrow, next week, or anytime soon. A good way to stay protected is to choose to invest in good companies that can easily survive, and grow beyond tough times. This is also a good time to sit on large amounts of cash, and wait for that day where the good stocks we like, and want go on sale.

CHAPTER 2.3: STOCK INVESTING RULES

W arren Buffett's, also known as "the world's greatest investor" multiple times have mentioned these investing rules:
- Invest on a company you know, and understand.
- Durable with a competitive advantage.
- With management that have integrity, and talent.
- And a price per share that makes sense.

A couple of tools that are out there to help us are the company's statements, annual reports, and company's strategies.

No matter how good a company is, it does not have an infinite value to be paid for. The secret is to buy it on sale, when the market is down, or an event has brought such a company value down, but due to our research we know that that company will grow back. Identifying good companies earlier in their life stages allows us to capitalize more. It's very hard to make money on a company that is already all the way in the top in value with no more room for growth.

A great approach is to make a list of the companies we like (it's much better to invest in a company you believe in, and are proud of), know and fully understand. Wait for these specific companies to go on sale, buying low, and selling high maximizing profits.

Once again, May 2019, is a great time to be sitting in large amounts of cash because the signs are too many to neglect.

At the current moment we can build a list of around 10 companies that we like, know, and fully understand, and wait for that moment those companies go on sale so we can buy.

If you are just starting this, you may ask how long it may take to learn all needed to never make mistakes, and the answer to that is that no one ever will know everything, but the secret is to start investing a small amount so you can practice with a few hundred dollars, and as time passes by (months, years) increase the investing amount, because if you never start, and learn what a stock looks like on sale, and how you feel and behave when you see the stock you hold price change you will miss the magic opportunity, or might buy something thinking it is something it actually is not. Accumulating knowledge is key to making good decisions.

In case you do not want to put in the time to learn, or if you do not trust yourself enough making such decisions, another solution is to invest in a 401k, or an Index fund, such as the S&P 500. This means you would be riding the market being invested in the top 500 US companies for example, which, average grows 9% percent a year, and not try to beat the market picking the top companies out there.

Another approach is to combine both worlds; of investing long term, plus putting it inside a retirement account, Roth IRA, and still pick the winning companies that you know have the strongest long term growth. All money made, and grown inside a Roth IRA account is tax free, but, for the most part you can only access it after age 59 and half.

Start investing small, few hundreds, while dealing with a learning curve, then you may transition into few thousands. Do not put all your money, or a high amount into something you do not know. A good time to start investing, and learn is today with smaller amounts of money, then later in life with bigger amounts, or smaller amounts.

CREDIT CARDS

Chapter 3: Cash Back and Credit Card Promotions

Lots of people hate credit cards, and avoid them at all costs, and I do not blame them. Credit cards can ruin a person's name when wrongly used, but, there is a place for credit cards, especially once you fully understand the system, and can make it start working in your advantage.

Let's get started:

The secret here is not to charge your credit card buying things you do not need, because you will get a small percentage back. You have to use your credit card every time that it is possible to buy things you were going to buy anyway, like food, groceries, house expenses, phone bill, gas, etc. Instead of paying cash for these things you swipe your credit card. Now you are getting that percentage (usually 1% – 6%) back, small?! Yes, but it's great since you were going to buy those things anyway like food, or your phone.

Equally extremely important is to pay the credit card in full at the end of the monthly billing cycle. This is the only way this strategy can fully work. If you do not make a full payment, and let the credit card bill snow ball into next month's bill that 1 to 6 percent that you were collecting means nothing, because the credit card company would then collect 15% to 30% off of you.

This is the reason, even though we are now buying everything with a credit card we still can only buy things that we could buy cash at that moment anyway.

This is the secret to go around the system. I have not paid one penny to credit card companies for over 5 years, and I collect about $200 yearly off my credit cards (I only use 2 credit cards at the moment). This revenue number could be so much higher if it was somebody else, but for me this number is ok, because I try my best to cut all my expenses, and only spend money on things that can generate more money, so at this point there is not that many things that I buy anyway.

Using a life minimalist approach I have been realizing that the amount of happiness a brand new expensive fancy shoes can give me is not worth the regret I end up feeling if had instead invested that money in an asset that could generate a meaningful return. By no means I am saying walk barefoot, or use shoes with holes on them, this is an example.

Only buy things with the credit card if you are able to pay for it with cash as well, because if you cannot afford it now, you will not be able to afford that bill next month when it will be piled up with that month's expenses plus the interest the credit company will be collecting off of you.

Now that we know all these strategies we need to find the best offer out there, and believe me there are many, I do not invest crazy amounts of time into this but my personal bank currently give me 3% cash back in an specific transaction type I choose (at the moment I chose online purchases), 2% cash back for another category, and 1% cash back for everything else. Plus I get another 75% increase if I transfer that cash back to a savings account with that same bank.

Credit cards collect a fee from merchants on every transaction. Another reason, banks can afford to offer great cash back deals is because the majority of people do not simply collect that cash back, but allow the bank to instead collect from them, and even worse, thinking that they will get their money back, go all out, and spend more than they would if they were not offered that cash back reward.

Another point to take in consideration are fees that the credit card may charge. If the cash back percentage is great, but the card charges monthly fees it might not be the best option, since there are so many fee free cash back credit cards out there for most people that would be the best way to go.

It is your choice and option to be the one colleting the benefits, or to be the one paying so others can collect these benefits. In reality if the majority of people followed the steps I suggest banks would stop these offers.

Let's go over these steps again:

1- Only swipe the credit card for things that you were going to buy anyway.

2- Only buy things with the credit card if you are able to pay for that item in full with cash at that moment.

3- Pay the credit card bill in full every monthly billing cycle.

4- Find the biggest percentage cash back credit card with $0 fees, or monthly fees.

Another credit card related point I will mention is that to attract new customers credit card companies offer, gift cards, travel points, and other perks for opening an account with them. After collecting your gifts, and bonuses, most of the time there will be no penalties if you decide not to use that account, or even close it. It is up to you to keep the credit card or not.

REAL ESTATE

Chapter 4.1: Crowed funding

C rowdfunding funds large projects collecting small amounts of money from a large amount of people. You may not be ready to buy your own home, or make a big real estate investment, but that doesn't necessarily mean you cannot invest in real estate. New technology, and new investing platforms are making easier than ever before to invest in real estate with less than $1,000.

Investments can be in apartment buildings, offices, retail stores, restaurants, and even senior houses. There are over 100 websites that allow you to invest in a portion of the real estate market, and you don't need a lot of money to get in. Even as little as $500 can get you started. Returns can be on the double digits.

Make sure you do your homework, some of these sites charge high fees, also, make sure there is an easy way out when you want to take your profits out, and leave.

Check out the location of the investments to make sure there is solid employment in the area, a good population growth, and high demand.

Chapter 4.2: Become a land lord

There are rental companies that help you find, purchase, and manage rental homes. They even help you sale the home when you want to get out. They do charge a fee.

Choose a location that is in high rental demand. A great way to go about this is to look at those very high demand areas, that often times are over inflated, but drive 5 to 10 minutes away from that specific location, but not too far away. Those types of spots, still with room for developing, and growing may offer you a more affordable deal, not over inflated, and still be in a high demand area since it is not far from where the action is happening.

Real state returns come both in rent, and in an increase in the home's value over time.

Make sure the rent you can charge is high enough to cover all monthly costs, which includes: mortgage, principal, interest, property taxes, homeowners insurance, repairs, and maintenance, and still allow cash flow.

Develop a down time saving, every couple of years you will get a month, or more without tenants, or transitioning to new tenants. Make sure to screen your to be tenants to prevent later in time unwanted surprises, or headaches.

Make sure you understand the area you will be investing. The area you grew up in is usually a good example of an area you understand. Visit as many homes as you can during the process of choosing the right home, make sure the area's economy is strong, and the local businesses are thriving, there are good schools, high demand, and the properties are not over inflated.

All this takes time to set up, but after finding the perfect unit, where the numbers make sense, finding good tenants, most months no extra work is required, but only collecting cash flow.

You could start with a duplex, live in one unit, rent the other unit, and have your tenant help you pay your mortgage. In a good economy after a few years you can start this process all over, and invest in a new duplex, for example, or something that makes sense for your specific location, and situation.

The laws vary from state to state, and even towns to towns, but usually a 20% down payment and a good credit score around the 700 will help getting good financing.

Chapter 4.3: REIT Stocks

A nother option is to buy a REIT stock, "Real Estate Investment Trust". These are groups of properties owned by
one developer.

REIT offer high dividends because they are required to give shareholders most of their profits.

There are REIT's for every type of real estate. Retail is not too hot now, because so much shopping is happening online, but warehouse REIT's for online companies are currently in high demand.

WRITE A BOOK

Chapter 5.1: Write a Book / Start Writing

The most sold books are fiction: romance, sci-fi, and fantasy. A second great market is non-fiction on any niche you are a specialist, or expert at. The more entertaining, or valuable the information, and content of your book the better.

Many of us always wanted to write a book, but always put it off, thinking it's too much work, or having no idea how to start. The best way is to just start writing. For me particularly laying down sub titles as the skeleton of the book, and then focusing on writing one chapter at a time works wonders. When just focusing on writing one chapter at a time, around 1k words, the job seems easier, and more doable. If we only think about the entire book, the task seems gigantic, terrifying, and impossible to be accomplished. Once we divide the work in parts it is much more manageable.

Finding a quiet place is helpful for most writers.

Another point that slows things down is trying to make it perfect the first time around; writing 4, or 5 words, and then backspacing a word, or 2 making sure it is all perfect. By now I have realized that that wastes time, and instead I just start writing, and keep writing letting all the ideas come out, and go into the paper, or screen. I leave many grammatical errors, commas, and rewording for later, making sure at that moment that the main ideas get written, or typed down before it slips away of the mind.

There will be plenty of time later to proof read, and reword to perfection, which, then will be much easier since the main ideas are already there. A book does not need to take a year, or years to be written, also it does not need to be gigantic. Smaller more affordable books, or series of books are fine as well instead of one huge, and expensive book.

Chapter 5.2: Publishing

Publishing costs, and complications were the reason I put off book writing for so long. Scared of all the costs involved, and how many book sales would be needed to generate a profit. But today there are ways around the publishing cost, and you can publish your book for free.

There are many institutions that will publish your book for free, the biggest one of them is Amazon KDP, Kindle direct publishing. KDP will make your book available, and let you keep up to 70% royalties of your book sales.

The more platforms you make your book available the bigger your audience can be; such as online electronic book, paper back, and audible.

Chapter 5.3: Marketing

You can write your book, make it available, and collect profits every time a sale is made. Your book is your asset that can generate income for you long term. It is a great experience, and achievement on itself.

You can let your sales just happen, or seek to maximize profits by advertising your book. How much marketing you want is entirely up to you:

- You can mention it on social media such as tweeter, and Facebook.
- Advertise on an email list.
- KDP offers free promotions.
- Make it free for a while to get people talking about it.
- Divide the content into smaller, more affordable books. More people will take a shot spending $1 to $5 instead of $10, or more. If they like one book they will come back for more.
- Make the book available in different languages.
- Book signing (traditional way). Can be at a book store, book festival, café, or anywhere.
- Run an eBook signing with digital signature using an autography app.

Marketing or not, or how much marketing is up to you.

START A BLOG

Chapter 6.1: Start a Blog and Run Ads

When Building your blog you can decide what you will make it about. You can choose an area that you are most passionate about. That way the time you spend on it will not feel like just another job. Also, how much time you put in is up to you, and when to put in the time is also entirely up to you. There are different ways you can make money in your webpage.

One way is to run ads;

- CPC/PPC Ads: cost per click (also called pay per click) ads are usually banners that you place in your content, or sidebar. You will get paid each time a reader clicks the ad.
- CPM Ads: CPM Ads pay a fixed amount of money based on how many people view the ad.

Google AdSense is the most famous one but there are many other ads programs out there. You do not choose which ads will show on your webpage. Google AdSanse will ask you, and find out what your webpage content consists of, and will display the appropriate ads to maximize clicks.

If the traffic on your webpage is big enough private companies will want to show their ads on your page directly. You can sell other people products, and collect a commission.

There is affiliate marketing, which consists of an advertiser giving you a unique link for you to place on your webpage, and every sale generated from that link on your webpage gives you a commission of the sale.

You may also sell, and advertise your own products on your blog, such as eBooks, online courses/workshops, images, video, music people can use in their own content, apps, or physical products.

To improve sales before creating these products, hear from your readers, and find out which products (content) will be useful to them.

Chapter 6.2: Making Your
Blog Most Effective

B uilding your own blog can give you credibility as you, and your page becomes bigger. This can create opportunities when somebody approaches you to co-author a book, speak in a conference, or run a training related to your niche.

-     There is no need to go all out with spending. There are affordable, and also free hosts to choose from.

-     Choose a topic you know, understand, and are passionate about or/and enjoy doing. This is what will keep you going on the long run.

-    Choose a domain name.

-    Choose a theme.

- Start an email list. Collecting the email of your loyal readers will help grow traffic to your page. This way whenever you write that great new blog post you know it will go viral.

As long as your content is good, entertaining, or useful traffic will grow, and you will be able to add meaningful monetization to your page.

YOUTUBE

Chapter 7.1: Create a YouTube Channel

You probably already have a YouTube account. The next step is to upload videos, and develop an audience. Once you have 4,000 watch hours in the last 12 months, and 1,000 subscribers you qualify to apply for monetization. As long as your channel content is genuinely yours, not plagiarizing, or showing illegal content YouTube will take you as a partner. Now you can start running ads from YouTube, and mention products for specific companies, or sell your own products, and collect money from all these sources.

Reaching 4k watch hours, and 1k subscribers does take some time, but once you are enrolled you do not need to keep meeting this threshold every year. As long as you are not inactive for over 6 months YouTube will keep your channel open, but for most people the start is the hardest since no one knows you. From 0 to 100 subscribers is harder than from 100 to 1,000, because there is now a base to work with.

You need to make a video once, and after that your video is available to be watched, run ads, generate views, and give you profits for years to come. Many YouTubers end up making You-Tube their full time job. Some use the platform as a part time, or a side hustle.

Here you will be your own boss, you can upload one video a

week, which may take 2 to 4 hours to make. You may also decide to put 1 video monthly, or daily. As long as you are talking about something that is meaningful to you it will not feel as a job, and you can actually enjoy what you will be doing. This creates options for you, and your future.

Chapter 7.2: Build an Audience

To grow your audience quality content is key. As long as the content is entertaining, or useful your channel will grow quickly.

There is no need to go crazy spending hundreds, or thousands buying equipment, which may cost from a few bucks to hundreds. The microphone, and camera you already have are fine to start. Software can also be costly, but you can choose the free options, especially to start, and see how you feel. You may also use YouTube video editing as another way of improving videos.

Make a channel that is visually appealing to stimulate clicks. Use attention calling thumbnails to increase clicks on each video you upload. High quality, and high resolution images are helpful. There are plenty of free webpages that offer free images for you to use in case you will need those instead of doing head talking videos.

Edit your images using the software of your choice. Uploading videos consistently that viewers like watching is ideal, once a week is a good pace, but you can do every other day, or monthly. Do follow a schedule to help you stay on track. You may, also create a welcome trailer for your channel page. Promote your videos on social platforms to get it started.

Be the face of your channel, and brand. It will help create trust for your viewers. Put your picture on your profile instead of a logo.

To reach the: 4k watch hours in the last 12 months, and 1k subscribers ask people to subscribe. You may say it, or if you feel that's intrusive you can edit it into your videos, so viewers will read the message to like, and subscribe as they hear you. By editing your call-to-action during your video, reminding your viewers to subscribe may be less intrusive.

CHAPTER 8: AFFILIATE MARKETING

With affiliate marketing you promote other people's products, and add a link to your page directing the buyer to the seller. Once the buyer clicks your link you will earn a commission from all items purchased throw your initial link. The link will be active for a specific time, such as 24 hours or so. This way the person selling the product increase sells buy sharing the profit.

If you want to sale your product you will offer promoters a financial incentive using the affiliate program, and if you do not have a product, and want to make money you may sale somebody else's product that you feel has value, and collect a profit as an affiliate marketer.

Amazon Associates is the most popular affiliate program. You can join them, and start earning commissions by promoting any number of the wide variety of products available on their platform. The sign up process is fairly quick, and easy. Amazon associates dashboard will give you all the tools to add banners, and share links on your own blog. Pick products that are popular, and will match your audience.

Other affiliate platforms are CJ Affiliate, Clickbank, Linkshare and Share a Sale.

CHAPTER 9: ONLINE COURSE OR GUIDE

Making money with online course is a field that's growing more, and more every year. First you will need to come up with a course idea, then develop the course content, and finally promote, and sell your course.

The most profitable online courses make up to $75k a year, and even $1M a year. But making $500, or $1k a month is a meaningful income for most people. You will need to develop the course once, but you will get paid by every new student that buys your course.

If you are a great teacher of a foreign language, or know gardening, or have stock market knowledge, or anything you are an expert at; you can teach that, and develop your course. In case you are not an expert in anything, or at least anything that there will be an audience willing to buy, another option is to learn as you go using research, and studying to develop your course. Pick a course topic that interests you, and read the 3 top selling books on that field. After that you become an expert, and will know more than most people that will be interested in your course.

Choose a topic that you are passionate about, and has a market, so you can make money selling it. Figure out a problem that people have, and build a course that solves that problem.

If you are not sure the topic you chose to build your course will sell well, you may ask people how they feel about it, ask more people than just close friends, and family. You may also send an email with a couple of lines mentioning some top points of your course, and see how people will react to it. A third way to find out if the topic you chose has potential is to set up an "apply to buy" page, that way you sell your course even before you are fully developing it.

Your first course will not be perfect, and gigantic but make it as good as possible considering it will be your first course.

- Create a clear outline of the topic you have chosen.
- Divide the course into 5 to 10 lessons.
- Each lesson have to be 5 to 10 minutes long to keep students engaged.
- Develop videos (of you, or your computer screen), text, and/or audio.

Most online courses consist of videos, and worksheets to help students apply what they learn. Good microphones, lighting, and video quality are great, but most important is how valuable your content will be to solve their specific problem.

After coming up with a course idea, developed the course content all you need to do is choose an online platform to make your course available for students.

Chapter 10:Rent Your Extra Space

Rent the extra rooms in your house. If you have the space, and are willing to put up with some noise this can work wonders. Many people have their room tenants pay their mortgages for them, or even living for free just by doing some managing.

A great approach to make this work is to make things as simple as possible. Make all utilities included, and charge a fixed weekly amount. In the case your electricity, or gas start getting too high instead of creating a complicated situation, or a fight just raise the rent you charge to cover the new extra specific needs of your tenants.

Ideally your tenants will rent your room because they are frugal, and will be saving, and investing their money, but there is a chance the reason for them to choose to rent a room instead of their own entire place is poor budgeting. It does not mean they do not make enough money, but there is a big chance they just miscalculate their spending. For this reason you want to charge your tenants weekly, this way they will pay you as soon as they get the money.

If based on your location, size of your house, and size of the room you are renting you decide to charge $500 a month, split it into weekly payments of $125. Or if your tenant gets paid bi-weekly charge $250 every other week.

Make sure you will be charging enough to cover all utilities. Including all utilities into the rent will require you to do some good budgeting, but it will make things much easier than splitting all house bills, and having different amounts to deal with every week, or month.

Compare how much you will be charging to how much others

charge in your area, by checking Trulia, or Craigslist, this way making sure you are competitive.

Decide if you can put up with having other people in your house, and if this path of income is for you. Interview people, and search/google for their names on the internet with spelling variations to prevent any later surprises. Set up house rules such as up to when noise is ok, and others.

Many areas renting rooms is just as fine as renting houses, or properties. But some locations the amount of unrelated people in a house becomes illegal after reaching a certain number. Check the laws of your area, and obey them to prevent later complications.

If you plan on doing this a lot, for many people, and many rooms that you have. Keep an attorney in mind, just in case someday you need it. Treat people well, with respect, and communicate clearly.

Another option now a days is Airbnb. To rent your room using Airbnb you will need to create an account with them. Set up your listing. List amenities, and describe your space accurately. List all your nearby attractions, and activities. Post good, realistic photos of your space to prevent guests being disappointed. Check your local laws, and regulations.

CHAPTER 11: BONUS (OWN, OR INVEST IN A BUSINESS)

Silent partner in a business

You can make/turn a business into passive income by being a silent partner. There are risks involved, as in any other business. Here you need to make sure your vision, and beliefs are aligned with your partner's. You would then be coming in with capital, but leaving running the business fully, or for the most part for your partner. You both collect profits, and are also, both responsible for the business.

Bonds: Invest in Business Using Bonds

Bonds are loans, that an investor provides the borrower, usually big corporations, or the government, and collect their money back with interest. When companies, or the government need to raise money for projects they will issue bonds. USA federal government bonds are considered the safest bonds since in case of a recession by the time the federal government fails, all the other companies and institutions in the country will by then be gone. Also, if needed the government, even though not a good thing, can always print more money.

Vending machines (restock, and collect the money every 2 weeks)

You will need to get the machines and find the locations. There is a big variety of vending machine types, including smaller gum-ball, other candy, drinks, snacks, healthy snacks, games, and others. You may start with one, or two machines of your desired size, and price, see how you feel about it, and scale it up with time. Another option is buying used machines on craigslist instead of brand new ones, making sure to get a good item (machine) for a more affordable price.

Finding good locations is helpful for great returns. After finishing setting it up; the machines will need to be restocked every other week, or so, and you can go collect your money whenever you want it. If the machine stops taking money, or the location owner calls you saying that the machine became empty sooner it is ideal to attend the machine, and refill it as soon as possible to increase profits, and keep the location owner happy. For this business to be extremely profitable, it will require time, and high scalability, meaning many many machines. Another option is to hire a person to attend your machines for you.

CONCLUSION

I advise budgeting;

1- and getting rid of all bad debt. Bad debt is the opposite of debt that generates income such as the mortgage from your rental unit that provides you with monthly cash flow.

2- Once debt free, save 3 to 6 months into your emergency fund. Emergency such as job loss, or sickness, not Macy's discount week, or the new iPhone 30. This money can go into your high APY interest savings account, and you will start seeing your money grow.

3- Debt free, emergency fund ready. Invest your money, maybe 401k retirement account, or a Roth IRA retirement account are great starts that provide great benefits.

4- I do not know what investment you like the most, but invest your money. Stock market, real estate, business, or some other investment you like.

You decide how much risk you are ok with. At my current situation in life, and 33 years old, I'm ok with a 20% return, and risk. These type of investments involve smaller risk, and a return high enough to be meaningful. Consult with your financial adviser, and take in consideration your specific situation before making any major decisions in your financial life.

Leaving saved money under the mattress means it loses its value at a 3% average annually to inflation for this reason investing becomes such a good idea.

Only you know what true happiness is to you. Personally investing time learning, and growing my financial knowledge, and knowledge in general gives me great peace of mind, and if you took the time to read this book it means you as well value information. Owing too much money, or having crazy debt is a stress that I highly avoid.

We get to choose, what to invest in, and if we even do want to invest. By being scared of failure and taking no risks will result in less failures, but by not trying will also result in less achievements. Imagine the results that can be accomplished by standing up, and taking a few risks. I am not ok with working 40 to 50 years of my life making my big corporation bosses beyond rich, and myself just be scraping by. A short term plan (4 months), a mid term plan (1 year), and a long term plan (7 years) provide achievable mile stones that together over time tell a successful story.

Thanks for acquiring this book, and taking the time to consume its information. If you choose to implement one of these strategies, or all of them, more power to you.

Take charge of your financial life. Only you have the power to make your life great!

www.ingramcontent.com/pod-product-compliance
Lightning Source LLC
Chambersburg PA
CBHW030738180526
45157CB00008BA/3221